HELP!

I'VE GOT A PRESENTATION COMING UP

the ultimate guide to stress-free presenting

by Caroline Hopkins

This book is dedicated to my former stage-struck self and anyone who has ever suffered when speaking in public or giving a presentation.

I hope this will put an end to the suffering

Introduction

So, you've been asked to give a presentation. What is your first reaction?

"Fantastic! I just love presenting and I can't wait to share my ideas with as big an audience as possible."

"Finally, I am going to have the opportunity to connect people with some great solutions that will really help them"

"This is a fantastic opportunity to showcase my work and influence people to join me in my cause!"

(accompanied by an enthusiastic air punch)?

Well, perhaps, but if you are like most people I have worked with it is more likely to be:

"Oh God! do I have to? Why me? I HATE presenting! It will be awful… remember last time?! I would rather die than give a presentation!"

(Actually, this last comment is quite common, according to several research studies, which rank fear of public speaking above fear of death).

Giving presentations has become part of our working lives and yet most people don't like doing it. In fact, they hate it. It takes time to plan, time to stress and worry about beforehand and time to recover afterwards (if they make it through alive).

People get caught up in the myth of 'the natural', believing that some people were born with the skills to stand up and speak, spontaneously, with flair. In my experience, nearly every 'natural' presenter I have met has learnt to present well or speak with confidence in public. Even speakers who are famous for their charisma – like Bill Clinton – acknowledge that they were unremarkable when they started out: they have learnt the skills of presenting and public speaking and used them until they *became* natural.

If these so-called 'naturals' can learn – so can you. Presenting well is not a gift bestowed on the few: it is a skill that you can acquire - you just need to know how… and that is what I want to share with you in this short book. The processes, mindset and ideas that will give you everything you need to give better presentations.

You will probably already know that the only way you are going to get better at presenting is by doing it. No book can do it for you. So, no surprise there, but… there is a hard way and an easy way to get experience.

The way most people go about it is by practicing their skills when there is a lot at stake. I am guessing that you wouldn't learn to swim by jumping off a cliff. So don't try and learn presenting by 'having a go' at a major client pitch. Or worse, presenting in front of your entire company at the annual conference. That is the hard way (believe me, I've tried it.)

The easy way then is to find opportunities to speak in public when there is not a lot riding on it. You need to start with the knowledge and information – which you will get from this book - and then use this straight away by giving presentations whenever you can, in situations that aren't too daunting. Maybe to a few friendly colleagues or warm clients… and build up from there until you feel ready to grab the mic and stride out with confidence at a 5000 seater conference. The sky's the limit when you have skill *and* experience.

I realise that you may have reached for this book because you *already have* a high stakes presentation lined up. Don't worry. You will still find plenty to help you in the pages that follow (and I am sure you will be fine on the day) – but I would still urge you to keep finding opportunities to speak frequently the 'easy way' so that you never have to worry about speaking in public again because you no longer fear or dislike it and you too will have become a natural.

"Presentation is the killer skill we take into the real world... it gives us an unfair advantage"

The McKinsey Mind

CONTENTS

"To be an impressive public speaker, you have to believe in what you are saying. And if you speak with conviction and you're passionate about your subject, your audience will be far more forgiving of your mistakes because they'll have faith that you are telling the truth. My answers aren't always smooth and immediate, and often include a fair few "erms" and "ahs" - but most audiences are far happier with a hesitant, sincere response than a speedy but superficial answer.

Prepare, then take your time and relax. *Speak from the heart.*"

Richard Branson, Founder & Chairman of Virgin Group

What makes a presentation successful?

There are hundreds of books, articles and ideas about effective communication and how to get your point across. But is that what a good presentation is about? Is it just about getting your point across?

Really great presenters do more than that. They engage, they connect with their audience and *they make them feel something* – whether it is feeling amused, sad, shocked, curious to learn more, motivated, validated, angry or a combination of all of these things (hopefully not all at once though). It is the *experience* the audience has which determines how they rate the presenter.

To do this well requires confidence in yourself, your material and your mission.

This is as true of a new business pitch (where you want them to feel a connection and desire for your product or service) as it is of a keynote conference address.

As a general rule of thumb, presenters who get the audience to laugh (hopefully with them, although 'at them' can also work in certain contexts) are usually onto a winner. Shared laughter is the ultimate rapport builder and most audiences will rate a presentation in which they have laughed as the mark of a competent presenter.

To reach this nirvana of presenting skill though is usually down to self-belief, boosted by masses of confidence that you know your stuff and you are familiar with your delivery.

On the way, you are likely to pass through several levels of competency as a presenter – and how quickly you move through the levels will depend on how often you present (and how quickly you learn!).

This ideas in this book will help you to get the basics right: to clarify your core message; to create content that brings your message to life; to manage your nerves and have the confidence to deliver your message well – so you can quickly start to reach high levels of skill as a presenter.

The key thing is that, wherever you are with this now, you continue to present and hone your skill and confidence until you really **love presenting**.

Session 1: Effective Planning

Session 2: Creating Your Content

Session 3: Make It Memorable

Session 4: Be Ready To Deliver With Confidence

"Be sincere; be brief; be seated."

Franklin D Roosevelt

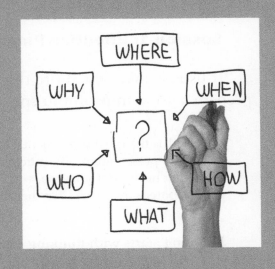

Session 1: Effective Planning

Session 1: Effective Planning

"It usually takes me more than three weeks to prepare a good impromptu speech." *Mark Twain*

Session 1 is the most fundamental to creating a successful presentation. By anticipating your audience well, their needs and situation, you will be more likely to create content that works for them and for you.

Planning starts with thinking – not writing slides.

This is the stage where you need to answer a few questions.

- **Why** are you presenting?
- **Who** is in the audience?
- **What** will you present?
- **Where** and **When** – the logistics of your presentation?
- **How** will you organize everything so you are ready?

To help you, this session includes 3 templates to focus your thinking and record your answers

❖ **Outcomes Matrix** to clarify win/win for you and the audience
❖ **Structure Template** to complete with your answers,
❖ **Logistics Template** to check all the details and to focus your thinking.

Also in this session, you will create your structure for your presentation – using a simple pyramid model.

WHY?

Why?
Know your outcome

Answer these questions to identify your outcome and write summary of this outcome in the top left hand box on page 15.

Why are you doing this?

- - - - - - - - - - - - - - - - - - - -

What will be a great outcome for you?

- - - - - - - - - - - - - - - - - - - -

Connect with your enthusiasm

Complete the following sentences and write a summary of your answer in the bottom left hand box on page 15

I am excited about this opportunity because...

- - - - - - - - - - - - - - - - - - - -

I think it will benefit my audience because...

- - - - - - - - - - - - - - - - - - - -

Outcomes / Interest Matrix

Your outcome (top left)

Put your outcome here	
Write here why you are passionate, enthusiastic or care about giving this presentation	

Your passion/enthusiasm (bottom left)

The next step is to think about your audience – so that you can complete the right hand side of the matrix... *who is in your audience?*

WHO?

Who is in the audience?

Whether it is a sales pitch or a conference keynote… find
out as much as you can before the day

Who are you presenting to and what will make it a good use
of their time? You need to do your research because you
will need to tailor your presentation accordingly.

Try to answer the following questions and then write your
summary in the matrix, as before:

**Why are they there? What is a good outcome for them
from being in the audience?**

- -

What is the profile of the audience? (their gender, age,
knowledge of your subject, attitude towards this topic, perception
of you and anything else you can find out beforehand).

- -

Which aspects of this topic are **most likely to interest**, motivate
or appeal to them? Where are they now (their 'Point A') and
where would they like to be (their 'Point B') and how can your
presentation help them get there?

- -

Outcomes / Interest Matrix

As with your own outcomes and enthusiasm, complete the matrix
by having considered what your audience wants from this
presentation and what is most likely to interest them about it.

Their outcome (top right)

| | Write here what you believe the audience want to get from this |
| | Write here what you think they will be most interested in about your presentation |

Their likely interest (lower right)

You can use this method to quickly think through
your presentation each time you have to present, by
identifying the key answers to the 4 quadrants.

WHAT?

What?

Having identified **why** you are presenting, **who** will be in the audience and used the Outcomes Matrix to consider what will be a good results for you and the audience, it is time to create your outline. What will you include? More importantly, what will you leave out?

Structure is very important in preparing your presentation. The 'pyramid structure' is very useful to create your structure quickly and clarify your thinking.

The important thing to remember is that people have a very limited capacity for how much information they can take in (let alone remember afterwards). This has been proven in hundreds of research studies on retention. So, you need to choose wisely and make sure that you select your strongest points and focus on these rather than trying to communicate everything you know about your subject.

The Pyramid structure

Here's how it works. First you need to identify your **key message**. This is your central point – or proposition – that you want to get across. **If you only had 10 seconds to speak, this is what you would want to communicate.**

Then, you need to decide what **3 points** you want to make to support your central point or key message. The 'power of three' is used a lot in presenting as it is proven (again, there is masses of research to back this up) the optimum number of points that people take in and remember.

Finally, you need to write your **Opening** and your **Close**. These are the two most powerful moments of your presentation. The opening because that is when people are being most attentive (and are also deciding whether to keep listening to you); and the close because this is what people are most likely to remember and take away as their impression of you. The close is also where you will make your **Call to Action** (CTA).

Having created your structure, you then decide what **Supporting Evidence** will strengthen your 3 points. This can be facts, research statistics, examples, case studies and other forms of visual or experiential proof. As a rule of thumb, allow up to 3 supporting facts or points for each of your key points.

At this stage, you also can think of ideas to make your opening more impactful with perhaps a powerful question or quote, props or an unusual fact that arouses people's interest. Finally, think about a **strong title** for your presentation or talk; particularly if you want it to encourage people to attend – something that will perhaps arouse curiosity while also indicating the theme and message of your presentation.

The figure below shows the pyramid structure. You can also use the Content Outline template on the following page to quickly create your pyramid structure each time you need to present. It will save you a lot of time.

Content Outline

Main message/ proposition:

Key Point 1	Key Point 2	Key Point 3
Supporting Arguments	Supporting Arguments	Supporting Arguments

Props/Exercises/Ideas to support the above points/arguments

Opening Statement/idea

Closing statement/call to action

WHERE? WHEN? HOW?

Where, When & How?

The **logistics template** on the following page will help you to make sure you have all the details surrounding your presentation and feel well prepared for the event.

As someone who is not good at small details, I find this list invaluable as a checklist to go through with the organizer to be confident that I have checked all the details. It also gives the organizer confidence in you – that you are professional and will be well-prepared.

How? is an equally important factor to consider as part of your preparation. You need to think about the following points:

- *How much time do you need*, realistically, to create your talk and source your supporting evidence, visuals and props? When will you timetable this in? What contingency time-slots can you also put in the diary?

- *Will you do everything yourself* or is there any part of the planning you can delegate to someone else – such as your slide creation, research tasks, organizational details?

- *When will you rehearse?* Do you want other people involved?

- *Is there any other help you need from others?* Input into your content – feedback, opinions or ideas? Do you want to arrange a group brainstorm session to create ideas? When will you involve others?

Logistics Checklist

Contact details of organisers:

Audience profile

Audio-visual facilities/soundchecks

Memory card/laptop required

Other speakers? Before/after me

Time allocated for my slot

Who will introduce me? Briefing required

Will there be a question session

Handout requirements

Delegate list

Layout of room/speaking area

Deadline for slides/handouts to be submitted

Marketing materials to take along

Directions/parking

Over To You: Start to Create Your Presentation

Based on the **Outcomes Matrix** and the **Content Outline** template, write the outline of your presentation, before moving on to Session 2 to start to flesh out your content and write your script.

Session 2: Creating Your Content

Session 2: Creating Your Content

"A wise man speaks because he has something to say; a fool because he has to say something." *Plato*

In this session we are going to **build on the outline** you created in Session 1 – the bones of your message – and develop the **content** of your presentation so you really connect and engage with your audience.

In Session 2 we will focus on:

❖ **Writing your presentation with AIDA in mind**

❖ **Brainstorming for ideas**

❖ **Anticipating questions & reviewing content**

Writing your presentation with AIDA in mind

AIDA is an acronym that has been used by the advertising industry for many years now as the requirements for a powerful ad.

It stands for:

A	Attention
I	Interest
D	Desire
A	Action

AIDA is a good test of your presentation content in making sure you have content that is going to have the desired effect on your audience.

A= Attention

You need to grab people's attention straight away. The good news is that this is when the audience is likely to be most attentive – when you start speaking. You need to make sure that you not only grab attention, but also reassure the audience that this is going to be worth their *continuing* attention.

You might want to think of it as a detonator: creating the initial energy of your opening few moments that makes people sit up and really listen… particularly if you are one of several presentations or keynote speeches. You want to stir people.

So, when you are planning your content, think about what will grab attention, what will be your detonator to get attention? It may be a question that makes people think, a prop or problem that arouses their curiosity or a story that they will find entertaining. Plan in your initial detonator and then aim to keep their attention throughout. How? Well that leads us on to…

I = Interest

Keep things interesting. You need to involve your audience, even if is by asking them rhetorical questions – and keep it varied.

This can be through your tone of voice, stories you share, props you introduce, exercises you give the audience to consider or actually do (maybe in pairs and then debrief their experiences). You can also vary things by sharing the stage with another presenter.

So as you write your content, think about how you will introduce new themes and ideas to keep things varied.

Another important consideration is the **'10-minute rule'** as defined by John Medina and his extensive research, which is described in his book 'Brain Rules'. Dr Medina is a developmental molecular biologist, who has conducted many studies on how the mind reacts to and organizes information.

The 10-minute rule reflects the amount of time we can concentrate before our mind starts to wander. It is important to us when we create our content because we need to make sure we introduce new ideas or move on to the next part of our topic every ten minutes if we are to keep the audience interested.

We also need to insert **'hooks'** into our presentation – between the ten-minute sections – so that we make sure we still have the audience with us, before moving on to the next part.

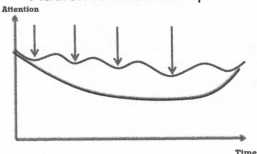

Audience attention spans

Ideally, a 'hook' will be something that breaks state or gets the audience to laugh – maybe an amusing story or example of your topic. This is the best way to keep their attention with you.

So, as you write your content, check that you have enough to keep it varied, with changes of theme or delivery every 10 minutes and enough 'hooks' in your material to involve, entertain and keep the audience wanting more.

Involving your audience

Involving your audience is key – so that they remain connected to you and your message rather than sitting as passive listeners in your audience. Good techniques to involve people are to:

- **ask questions (even rhetorical questions)**

- **ask for a show of hands**

- **arouse curiosity through a problem or momentary confusion which is quickly resolved**

- **give an exercise or ask them to do something together**

D = Desire

This is based on your understanding of your audience and what they want. What is their **desired outcome** or **'Point B'**? You need to make reference to this outcome or desired situation throughout your presentation and importantly, **how your proposition or call to action can help them to achieve this outcome.**

Phrases such as *'and what this means to you is...'* or **'Why is this important to you if you want to have X?'** can be used to keep your audience focused on their needs *and your solution to those needs.*

There is something called 'seeding' – particularly in sales presentations - which is where you build up to the solution you are going to be proposing by 'seeding' throughout what needs to happen to satisfy the audience's desired outcome, before you reveal your proposed solution and how it meets these needs.

A = Action

Be specific about what action you are proposing and HOW people need to act if they want to achieve their desired situation.

This is your Call To Action – don't bury it. Be very clear about it. Particularly at the end (or towards the end) of your presentation, you need to state your case or proposed solution and be direct about the next steps you want people to take.

Why people stop listening

Being aware of the reasons can help you to counter them. The key ones are:

- the presentation (or a section of it) is too long

- lack of audience participation creates 'sleep' mode,

- confusion or lack of understanding (and no opportunity to check understanding)

- the presentation meanders or has no structure

- the speaker's voice is monotonous

- distractions

- not interested in the subject – no clear relevance to the audience

Brainstorming for ideas

A great presentation is based on great thinking... and also some good ideas; which will add interest to your content, your presentation themes and provide colour and interest.

You may need to brainstorm ideas – even if it is only you attending the brainstorm session – which is often the situation for many presenters.

Whether you are brainstorming alone or in the company of other people, there are a few guidelines to bear in mind to get the most from your creative sessions.

There are **3 stages** to effective brainstorming – although most people stop after stage one. These are:

1. **Idea generation** – the more the better and no evaluation should happen at this stage as it can stifle creative thinking

2. **Judgment** – once you have a long list of ideas – written as headline summaries rather than long descriptions – you need to apply your critic at this point and pick what you think are the best ideas

3. **Closing the gap** – take your best ideas so far and consider how you might improve them to make them even better

Brainstorming 'rules'

- No premature evaluation – all ideas count

- The more ideas the better at the idea-generation stage

- Headline ideas to encourage flow

- Remember, it is a 3-stage process

Anticipating questions & reviewing content

Anticipating questions is critical to your preparation. Considering the likely questions the audience may have will help you in two key areas:

1.   Based on what questions you anticipate, you may decide to build the answers in to your content – especially if you think they will be important to the audience – and pre-empt them

2.   You will be able to consider good answers while you are relaxed, rather than thinking of answers when you may be feeling under pressure at the time of your presentation.

In any Q & A session, there will be questions that you will not have anticipated, but you will have a big advantage if you have considered your answers to the obvious ones.

A good technique for anticipating questions is to play 'If I Were In The Audience' and think about what you might be asking yourself or what questions you might want answered if you were in the audience.

<u>Over To You</u>: Create Your Content

Using the outline you created in Session 1, apply the ideas in this session to write your presentation – the script that you will deliver. Consider **AIDA** and **brainstorm** ideas to grab *attention*, keep the *interest*, seed the *desire* for your proposed solution and identify your call to *action*. Also, remember to use the **'10-minute rule'** to keep things punchy. Finally, think about what questions may come up.

Session 3: Make It Memorable

Session 3: Make It Memorable

"The success of your presentation will be judged not by the knowledge you send but by what the listener receives" *Lilly Walters*

By now, you will have created the structure and written your presentation. In Session 3 we are going to focus on what will **enhance your presentation** even more.

We are going to explore

❖ **How to help people to remember your message**

❖ **Creating powerful slides and visual aids to enhance your communication**

❖ **Stories, examples and props to bring your message to life**

❖ **The final cut: reviewing your flow and editing down**

❖ How to help people remember

We have already covered the 'Rule of 3' and how important it is to prioritise your content into a few points to make it memorable. People will only be able to remember one or two things about your presentation (if they remember anything at all!) and therefore you need to decide *what you want those 1 or 2 things to be.*

Ask yourself,

What is most important about your topic that you want them to remember?

A lot of research has been done into the field of memory and attention spans, which has revealed that people will notice or pay most attention to:-

- Messages at the start of your talk
- Messages at the end of your talk
- Messages that are repeated
- Things that are unexpected or unusual

This is shown visually in the graph on page 43. The blue line is the typical path of someone's attention in the audience. Notice, the curve is highest at points 1 and 4 (opening and close) but that it dips in the middle. Point 2 where the speaker introduced something unexpected and made people notice. The red lines at point 3 are where the message was repeated.

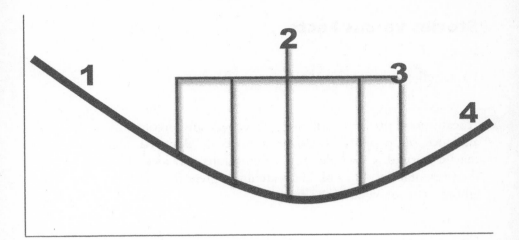

Audience attention spans

Attention will vary from person to person, but the key thing to remember, as the presenter, is that you need to use all 4 of these points if you want to make most impact, particularly to drive home your key message.

Stories versus Facts

Facts tell, while stories connect.

A really good presenter will not only engage and involve the audience, but people will also *feel* something. Amused, angry, sad, maybe worried… a whole range of emotions may kick in during the presentation. It's a bit like watching a great film, we get emotionally involved in the story.

Even the most banal or factual talk can become a hot-bed of emotional reaction if you link it to compelling *stories* about the issue.

Connecting with people's emotions has a far more powerful effect than merely spewing out logic, if you want to make a lasting impact and help people to remember your message. You connect with emotions through stories. Sharing experiences and human-interest stories (we call them 'human-interest' – they *interest us* as humans) that connect the audience with the experience of the story.

We can empathise with stories far more easily than remember facts.

Think about a good presentation you have been to recently… and notice what you still remember. Even if you don't consciously recall the details, you will probably remember stories the person shared with you, the big picture or gist of what they explained.

There is an exercise I often do in workshops where I will tell a story about a friend of a friend who suffered bad presenting nerves until they had a near-death experience.

I then go into the detail of the story and the result of the experience. In the same session I will share a mission statement of a well-known company and read it out to them. At the end of the session, I ask them to tell me what they remember about the story and the mission statement. Guess which they remember (and can recall in detail)? Always the story.

So use stories as much as you can. For each important message, think of a story, a case study or real-life example that illustrates this point.

The characteristics of a great story is that they introduce a character, who has a challenge or problem or difficult situation to face, who resolves the problem and triumphs (or as a warning story, doesn't resolve the problem and perishes).

Tips on using stories

- the story must be relevant in some way to your presentation

- don't brag - there is a big difference between telling people 'how great you are at everything and how much you have achieved' (which they may see as arrogance) with sharing a problem that you overcame (and allowing them to make their own judgment) which makes you seem more human.

- try to convey the **emotion** of the situation to your audience to build empathy (even if they haven't also won the lottery, they can relate to **the feelings** you describe)

- keep it short and punchy – no more than a couple of minutes

- rehearse it so you can tell it well - have a 6-7 point 'skeleton' of your story to prompt you

- stories go down well when they have been primed by a fact or piece of information

- explain the relevance of the story to the point you are making

Make STARS of your stories

To help you remember and prepare good stories, think of the acronym **STARS.**

S   **Situation**

T   **Task (or problem)**

A   **Action**

R   **Result**

S   **So what?**

This is a useful way to structure the telling of your stories. Start with the character (or yourself as the character) in the story and relate the **Situation**. Then explain the **Task** they had to face, the problem or issue that they needed to address (which is relevant to your message).

Next, tell us the **Action** they (or you) took to overcome this problem or address this issue (again, this will be relevant to your message or the call to action you are proposing). Finally, outline what happened as a **Result** and the implications of this story – the **So what?**

You may want to have a go now at trying a STARS story. Grab a piece of paper and write STARS down the left-hand side. Now take one of the themes or messages from your presentation and think about a story that illustrates your point – particularly one where the Action and Result are linked to your message.

As an example, let's say I was giving a presentation about speaking and wanted to illustrate the point that 'there is no such thing as a natural', I could use the story of Bill Clinton.

Bill Clinton STARS story:

Situation: In his autobiography, Bill Clinton admits he was not a great speaker in the early days. In 1988, he spoke at the Democratic National Convention, which was his national debut as a speaker.

Task: Unfortunately, Clinton's speech was quite boring. According to a TV reporter, Tom Brokaw, "He droned on and on and on. When he finally said 'In conclusion,' people began to cheer."

Action: Clinton quickly realized he didn't give his best performance. He knew how badly he'd done. Clinton bounced right back and talked to the media, and even made an appearance on that night's Johnny Carson's show.

Result: He wasn't great but he kept on going… he faced up to his poor performance and learnt to do it better next time. Today he is widely acclaimed as one of the best ever speakers. A natural.

So what? Presenting well is a skill we can all learn. Everyone has presentation 'bad days' but you need to keep going and learn from the experience. As we all know, not only did Bill Clinton recover from a very poor performance, he went on to become president.

❖ Creating powerful slides and visual aids

Slides and visual aids should add to your overall presentation and enhance the impact of your message. But, as we have all experienced, very often they are dull, confusing or distract attention away from the presenter.

The first decision to make is whether to use slides. You may decide to present without them and introduce ideas, stories, props and flip charts to illustrate your message.

If you decide to use slides, make sure they add value rather than distract.

Here are a few guidelines:

- **no more than 1 idea per slide** keep it easy for the audience to absorb your point

- **headline your slides with your message,** rather than subject headings, as this creates far more impact and gets your point across.

For example, 'Child Poverty Must End' is a far more powerful headline for a slide than a subject heading like 'Child Poverty'.

- **keep your slides as visual as you can**: use charts to illustrate changes or statistics or better still, convey your figures by using visual ideas that represent their significance. Use your own pictures or photo library images to add impact.

Dame Sue Ions, in a recent interview, was talking about wind farms and how the number of wind turbines needed to provide the power of a nuclear plant would fill an area the size of Greater London. This was a very visual image and I could instantly grasp the idea. As a slide you could take an image of Greater London and fill it with wind turbines to show this visually rather than just using numbers.

- **<u>DON'T</u> treat your slides as word pages** and fill them with text (particularly text which no one can even read) – this is what people mean by 'Death By Powerpoint'. It's a form of torture that, after a while in a dull presentation, makes death seem appealing.

- use each slide to **reinforce what you are saying** so that it complements your words rather than distracts from them

- **plan on paper first**: write a headline and sketch/decide on your visual for each slide. This makes it quicker to create the slides and source images.

- when using powerpoint, decide on your themes and colour scheme first and then keep it consistent. The simpler, the better.

- less is more – fewer words per slide, less clutter in your design, less confusion about the point you are making. Think simplicity.

Good Sources for pictures

The following websites are good for pictures to illustrate your slides. To save time, think first about what would be a good image and then search for that picture.

- www.google.com/images is great for ideas and seeing what you could use to support your message visually. For example, if I wanted to make a point about 'Presentation is a killer skill', I could put a search like 'microphone weapon' into google images and then trace the picture to a photo library to pay copyright.

- photo libraries are also a good source of pictures – some are free (eg. www.freerangestock.com) and some you pay to download images (eg. www.istockphoto.com).

❖ Using props to bring your message to life

For the full sensory hit, you can use props or special effects to demonstrate or provide another level of sensory experience to the audience.

I have been in presentations where they blacked out the room to demonstrate how it would be to be blind; thrown balls into the audience to convey the point about their message getting across and called up volunteers to demonstrate a technique in action and how it can be applied by the audience. All were very effective.

Brainstorm ideas around what you could use to add life to your message in the form of a prop, demonstration or exercise.

A few guidelines on using props well:

As with stories, make sure the prop is always relevant to your message (the audience should understand exactly *how* it is relevant)

Test your demo or rehearse well with the prop so it is seamless in the flow of your presentation – you want to be sure it will work on the day

Don't overdo props – the fewer the better to make an impact

Keep it simple – don't over-complicate things

Have a back-up in case your prop or demo doesn't work

Make sure everyone in the audience can see it (if you are using slides, put a large visual of the prop on your slide as you use it)

Put the prop away once you have finished with it so it doesn't distract from your next part of the presentation

❖ The final cut: reviewing your flow and editing down

As with any professional production, the final stage of creating your presentation is to edit your material. You need to be fairly ruthless in your assessment of what is strong enough to stay in, based on the principle that, when it comes to powerful communication, **less is more**.

Having decided on how you will add interest, you need to review how your presentation flows – check you are happy with the order of your points and move things around if necessary so you have a powerful talk, which communicates your message clearly and will achieve your intended outcome.

The Grandma Test

The Grandma test is a good measure of your clarity and meaning. If she were in the audience, would she understand it? Would she be able to tell you what your central point or message was?

<u>Over To You</u>: Add interest to your presentation

Think about your key messages: if people only remember one or two things, what do you want them to be? **Write it down.**

Review your presentation content. Have you made good use of the **opening** and **close** to make your point? Do you repeat your key message during the presentation? Can you do anything to make your message more memorable? Props? Audience experience? Stories? Video or audio clips? Powerful statistics conveyed with visual comparisons?

Write down what else you can use to add life to your message.

Will you be using **slides?** What are the headlines for your slides? What would make a good visual for each headline? Can you use charts or visual representations to convey your figures? When will you create your slides – can you delegate this to anyone or outsource the job?

What **stories** can you use to support your key points? What is the relevance of these stories to your message?

What concrete evidence or examples of your messages can you create for your **props** or **demonstrations**? How can you source these or what do you need to do to set them up?

Finally, what can you cut out, cut down or improve? Review your script to cut out anything that dilutes your core message. Subject your presentation to the Grandma test – would she get it?

By now, you want to have your content ready, with your ideas to add interest and memorability in hand – so that you can start to learn your script and rehearse your presentation, which we will be covering is Session 4.

Session 4: Getting Ready To Deliver With Confidence

Session 4: Getting Ready To Deliver With Confidence

> "Confidence is the greatest friend" *Lao Tzu*

Session 4, our final session, covers how to **rehearse** and **mentally prepare** so you are confident and feel ready to deliver this presentation.

In this session, you will learn a few tips on **good delivery**, including the importance of your **body language** to enhance your communication, and how to follow through after your presentation.

In Session 4:

- ❖ **Learning your words**

- ❖ **Mental preparation**

- ❖ **Managing your nerves**

- ❖ **Getting into rapport**

- ❖ **Stage presence – the words, music and dance of powerful delivery**

- ❖ **Handling questions**

- ❖ **Follow-up and review**

- ❖ **Learning your words**

So, you have your presentation ready. It is well structured, makes your point clearly, is easy to follow and has enough ideas to keep it interesting... all you need to do now is learn it!

Many people I work with worry that they will not remember what they want to say. There is a great quote by American actor George Jessel,

"The human brain starts working the moment you are born and never stops... until you stand up to speak in public."

The key thing to remember is that you DO NOT need to learn exactly what you plan to say – the audience will not know if your remembered accurately or not. The exception is your opener and your close – which you should learn word-perfectly – and the rest you can learn using the following technique which I use myself and with my clients.

The 4 Steps To Learning Your Words

1. Read through your entire script, saying every word. Do not skim read or paraphrase what you will say at that part – *actually read it out*.

2. Take a highlighter pen and highlight or underline the key words in each sentence (just a few in each sentence) and read through again just looking at the key words. Then remove all the non-key words.

3. Remove further words until you just have one or two key words for each phrase or paragraph. Rehearse again. If at any time you can't remember (because you have removed too many words) you can go back and remind yourself of what you meant to say at that point.

4. Finally, transfer your skeleton key words to cue cards and rehearse a final time for fluency and this time include your props, or other ideas you plan to use in your presentation.

By this stage, you will have rehearsed four times, which may seem a lot but is the most effective way to imprint your presentation in your memory.

Word-perfect opener and close

The reason it is important you learn your opener and close perfectly is that the opening is when the adrenaline is likely to be at its peak. Given that you need to start strong and with confidence, you must be fluent in your opening remarks.

The close needs to be fluent and word-perfect because this is when you will deliver your final call to action or statement of your key message. It is what people will remember about your presentation – their final impression – so you need to make it powerful and be confident you know your lines.

❖ Mental preparation

Remember, there is no such thing as a natural. Even very experienced presenters will be apprehensive before a presentation, although they may appear calm. The difference is practice (ie. presenting often) and how they prepare – mentally and practically - before standing up to speak.

It is essential that you get into *the right state* and not *'a right state'*

Start liking audiences

There are several techniques below that will help you, but an important point to bear in mind first is your perspective: how you perceive the audience. Do you think of them as a hostile group of cold, staring faces – or as a group of people you want to get to know you better through your presentation.

This is important because it feeds into a lot of other self-talk that will either support or destroy your sense of comfort in front of the audience. Liking audiences, as a mindset, is a great starting point to feeling comfortable presenting to them.

There are a few exercises on the following pages that will also help with your mental preparation:

- **mental rehearsal**

- **challenging your beliefs**

- **state anchoring**

❖ Mental rehearsal

By mentally rehearsing – playing through in our mind how you want things to go - you are creating an experience of what you want to happen, rather than what you don't want to happen. Usually, when we are apprehensive about something, we *mentally rehearse* naturally except we play through all the negative scenarios of what might happen.

This mental rehearsal technique, described on page 61, encourages you to consider things going well instead.

Mental Rehearsal

1. Think about the presentation you have coming up and where you are likely to be when you stand up to present.

2. In your mind, imagine you are watching yourself as an observer, as if you were watching a film of yourself giving this presentation, from before you start, as you deliver your presentation right to the end where the audience reacts and you finish. 'Rewind' the film back to the beginning in your mind.

3. Watch the film again, this time making improvements in your behaviour – before you start presenting, as you deliver your presentation and finish speaking. Notice the different responses of other people each time you improve your performance. Rewind the film again and keep doing this as many times as you need to in order to produce the most excellent performance that you can.

4. Now that you have created a film of the most excellent performance possible, imagine you have stepped into the film and this time replay the film as if you are actually in it, seeing things through your own eyes, and performing this presentation from within your own skin and *become aware of what it feels like to perform this well.*

5. At the end of presentation, rewind the film and make more adjustments to your posture, gestures, tone of voice, content of your words, to improve your performance even more. Repeat this process until you feel sure that this is now your absolute best performance.

❖ Challenging unhelpful beliefs

This is a useful exercise to help you overcome your negative beliefs about the presentation you have coming up. It is sometimes called 'Angels & Demons' because it requires you to bring into your awareness what thoughts and beliefs you have about this presentation and your skill as a presenter - and encourages you to focus on the 'Angel' or positive messages rather than listening to the voice of your 'Demon'.

Grab a sheet of paper and write a line down the middle. Then, in the left hand column write down all the worries and concerns you have about this presentation. You will probably be able to think of a few.

If you are like most people who find presenting stressful, the chances are you have a list of uncomfortable thoughts, like:

> *"I wish I didn't have to do this – I hate presenting"*
>
> *"What do I know about XX anyway – they will think I am a lightweight"*
>
> *"They are all very high-powered business people, who am I kidding if I think they will consider me worth listening to"*

In the right hand column you now right down a counter-thought to each of these beliefs, which **could also be true** *and* which is far more useful to focus on if you want the presentation to go well. So, in relation to the thoughts above, these might be:

> *"This is a big opportunity to get better at presenting – I am well-prepared and want to really enjoy it"*
>
> *"I will make sure that by the time I present, I know my stuff really well"*
>
> *"I will be worth listening to because I have made the effort to make this interesting and relevant to these high-powered people"*

The first time I used this exercise it had a dramatic impact on my confidence. I was dreading a session that I was to deliver to a group of very senior medical consultants. When I did the exercise and pulled out my thoughts I realized I was terrifying myself! Who would want to endure the situation that my list was describing. So I 'countered' or challenged every belief. When I read the list down the right hand column I felt empowered and confident to do the session.

What Am I Telling Myself When I Stand Up To Present?

Negative belief	Relative (more useful) belief
1. I hate presenting	I am going to enjoy this today because I am really well prepared
2. They will think I am a fraud	By the time I present I will know my stuff and I will be myself when I present
3. I might forget my words and then I'll look stupid	If I forget my words, it is not the end of the world. I will have my cue cards and will just check my place
4. I always get so nervous – people will think I am rubbish	I am prepared, I have a great presentation AND I am going to give it my best shot. I think people will enjoy my presentation.
5. I wish I didn't have to do it	This is a good opportunity for me. It means I can apply my new skills at presenting AND I will be able to tell everyone about our new XYZ products and how great they are.

Notice how your energy shifts when you focus your attention on the more empowering beliefs on the right hand side. You enter a far better state to deliver your presentation.

Remember: What we focus on becomes our reality.

❖ **State Anchoring**

The final mental preparation exercise can be used before the day and on the day itself – as you stand up to present.

If you practice this anchoring technique a few times before the presentation then, on the day itself, you can imagine you have stepped into your ring of confidence as you walk up to the place you are giving your presentation.

Your Ring of Confidence

1. Imagine you have a ring of confidence like a spotlight on the floor, which you can step into at any time... When you step into this ring you can access the feeling of confidence

2. Identify the time when you most intensely experienced feeling really confident. Step into your imaginary 'ring' as you recreate the experience, as though you were there. Notice what you **See** (people, objects, colours), what you **Hear** (sounds, internal and external voices, silence) and what you **Feel** (emotions, sensations, locations, strengths.) Allow the feeling of confidence to grow and enjoy the sensation of confidence.

3. Break your concentration by stepping back out of the ring and bringing your attention back to the room

4. Repeat the process by stepping back into the ring and feel your confidence grow.

5. Step back out and pick up your ring – throw it down in a different spot and repeat the experience.

❖ Managing your nerves on the day

Feeling well prepared, knowing you have a good presentation, which you have rehearsed, is a huge help for your confidence on the day.

There are physical exercises you can do before presenting to warm-up and release any tension. Before we get into these though, a word on adrenaline.

What we experience as nerves – either before we start speaking or even during our presentation – increased heartbeat, tingling or shaking arms and legs, shaky voice, is all caused by adrenaline in our bodies. It is a very natural response, which everyone gets however experienced they are at public speaking.

The big difference between a confident performer and a nervous one is the interpretation of what these sensations *mean*. An experienced presenter who will stand up and appear confident will interpret the physical symptoms of adrenaline as 'normal' and even a sign that they are ready to start.

A nervous presenter interprets these physical sensations of adrenaline as scary, unpleasant and even as proof that they are not good presenters.

There is a story, told by Anthony Robbins about his experiences with two huge names on the international stage: Bruce Springsteen and Carly Simon.

Bruce Springsteen was a long-time hero of his, who Anthony Robbins was excited to personally meet. He asked whether, after all these years as a rock star he still got the same buzz from performing. Springsteen's answer was...

*"You know, Tony, when I am about to go out there, on stage, I get this electric feeling that starts in my chest and runs down my arms, my legs until my whole body feels alive — my heart is pumping fast and I **know I'm ready**... I'm pumped... and I go out there and give the performance of my life".*

Around the same time, Robbins got a call from Carly Simon, the international singer, who was suffering from bad stage fright. He asked her to describe her symptoms, which she did as follows:

*"When I am about to go on, I get this feeling in my chest, my heart starts to pound and I can feel my arms getting really shaky and my whole body starts to feel shaky and I **know I'm having a panic attack**... and I can't go out there."*

Exactly the same physical symptoms of adrenaline — pounding heart, tingling in the arms that spreads to the whole body — that cause Bruce Springsteen to **know he is ready** to give a great performance, cause Carly Simon to **know she is having a panic attack** and can't perform.

Last week, I was in the audience at a conference when the presenter asked us to call out our answers to his question. I am used to standing up and giving presentations myself and although I still get adrenaline when I present, it doesn't affect me as it used to. However, when the speaker walked over to where I was sitting and asked me for my answer, I noticed my heart was doing about 160 beats a minute and my body felt like I was going to run a sprint. I gave my answer confidently but inside I was running a powerhouse of adrenal energy.

Another important point about nerves and performance is that often we compare what we **see** in others *on the outside* with what we **experience** ourselves *on the inside* – and, believe me, we always come off worse. We can't see the adrenaline pumping round *their* body or the self-doubt that is whirring through *their* minds – we just see the exterior behavior. It's a bit like a swan we see gliding gently over the water, while below the surface a frenzy of activity is happening to create the motion.

When we compare what is happening on the inside for us with what we see on the outside in others… we are bound to come off worse.

How to manage when the adrenaline kicks in

1. Adrenaline creates a natural, physical reaction – which everyone gets – that you can counter by managing your breathing (deeper, slower breaths) and, if you can, physically shaking out the adrenaline, stretching out or moving

2. Be confident in your message – by having a point of view that you are keen to share, or a message that you want to be heard. If you can connect to your passion for your message, it will do wonders in overcoming your nerves when you feel the adrenaline

3. Remember, we need adrenaline to give our performance an edge. Without it, we would be flat and people wouldn't necessarily have the same desire to hear what we have to say. Adrenaline is exactly the same physical reaction as being incredibly excited about something – a holiday or exciting news – notice it and accept it as it will subside

4. Think about the story of Bruce and Carly – they had the same adrenal response but it had very different *meanings* for them - the key is to feel your adrenaline 'rush' and just **observe the symptoms of it** without making it mean something that stops you presenting well

5. Challenge your thinking – using the exercise on page 64. You can do this whenever you catch yourself having a negative perspective (even without writing it all down) – just mentally start countering your thoughts with the perspective of your more resourceful self

6. Know your stuff – so you feel confident about your material and will be more likely to present even when you have got adrenaline rushing through you

7. Shift your focus onto the audience – this presentation is really about them, not you, giving them an experience that will benefit them

8. Practice 'anchoring' your state using the Ring of Confidence exercise on page 65 so you become expert at creating an experience of confidence

❖ Authenticity

Always aim to be yourself when you give a presentation, albeit a slightly amplified version of yourself. Presenting is not acting – it is about connecting with others from a place of authenticity.

Some speakers have very good technique but we don't connect with them as they are not authentic and don't move or inspire us.

A speaker I heard recently had overcome a bad stammer and still spoke fairly haltingly but – because he was courageous and speaking from the heart – he won the audience over straight away.

You do not need to be a body language expert to pick up authenticity – you just feel it. So be mindful of having good technique in terms of the words, music and dance of your presentation, but always let your personality and passion through.

Mary & Martha

There is a film, 'Mary and Martha' by Richard Curtis, about two women who have lost their sons to malaria. In the film, Mary has an opportunity to speak in front of a panel of US Senators to make a case for funding to immunise against malaria. She has prepared extensively and arrives with various charts and arguments.

The judge throws her off balance by commenting that she isn't an expert and can only offer a personal opinion. She is momentarily floored until Martha intervenes and offers to show a few 'snaps'. She then gives the most heart-rending account of the people in the photos, ("this is Oliver, he likes to play the clarinet") which she spreads across a large table before telling the judge that very child in the vast spread of photos is now dead through malaria.

It is very powerful. Not slick, but raw... and very moving. It goes back to the point made in session 2 – we are interested in facts, *but persuaded through emotion,* which comes from authenticity rather than slick delivery.

❖ Starting Strong

Your opening is important, because people are forming impressions about you and deciding whether to keep listening.

When you start, your audience is likely to be 'cold' - this is why so many acts and performers use a 'warm-up' artist – to get the audience warm for their entrance. (I'm assuming you won't have a 'warm up' act!) Your energy therefore needs to be switched up a notch – so you are more energized and animated than the audience to create energy in the room

This is why you need to create a good 'opener' which you have rehearsed and can deliver with confidence as you know it word-for-word.

A few other ideas about your opening moments:

• **Find a face – however big the audience,** find a person and for a moment pretend that you and that person are the only 2 people in the room and just focus on them. Then, as if you were chatting, strike up a conversation with them. When you chat, you don't present. You don't transmit... You engage.

• **Flip your awareness** away from yourself and whatever adrenaline is pumping through your body to the audience. Really notice who is in the audience, who you are addressing and what appeals to you about this particular group (see 'start liking audiences' on p59). Shifting your awareness has two advantages: it takes the focus off your self-consciousness (literally) and it helps you to get into rapport because you are being fully present to the audience.

- **Act as if you are enjoying this** (if you are not actually enjoying it yet). If you were acting a part and wanting to communicate enjoying this, what would your facial expression be, your movement, your posture, your state. Get into this 'part' and before long you will start to loosen up... and your audience will warm up as they will consider themselves in safe hands. This isn't denying your authenticity but accessing the part of you that is fun, warm and likeable.

❖ Getting into Rapport

A few tips on getting into rapport with your audience. The essence of rapport building is getting people to connect at a level of like-ability or sameness. We are naturally in rapport when we establish things we have in common with another person: whether it is shared behavior, shared ideas and opinions or shared backgrounds and accents. In essence:

'people like people like themselves'

In conversation with one or two people, it is far easier to get into rapport because you can quickly identify shared experiences, beliefs, values and even match each other's body language... but it is far harder to establish what you have in common with a room full of people.

At a presentation level, you need to create rapport by getting the group into rapport with each other so you can join in the shared bonding. So, how do you do this?

Here are a few tips:

- **Your state** is key to building rapport. Your audience needs to feel they are in safe hands and respect you as the rapport leader. Start strong, project confidence (even if you don't feel it straight away), be loud enough to command attention.

- **Humour** is a huge factor is getting into rapport. Use any opportunity to get the audience laughing if it is appropriate to your theme – clearly not a good one for announcing redundancies or upsetting news – but for most presentations, if the audience have laughed frequently they have enjoyed the experience and will be grateful to you for that.

- As with humour, try to find other **universal experiences** or ask rhetorical **questions they are likely to agree with** to establish some commonality between you.

- Any **physical activity** that gets people acting together helps to get them bonding and in rapport with each other – maybe through a group activity, a show of hands or even clapping in unison.

❖ Stage presence – the words, music and dance of powerful delivery

Not just for the stage, but also to have presence in any situation where you are communicating, you need to be aware that your actual words are just a small part of your overall communication.

Of the three areas, the 'dance' or non-verbal aspects of a presentation has been proven to have most impact on an audience. This includes eye contact, your posture or stance and other non-verbal signals that people notice when they are in the audience, but often neglect when they are the presenter.

Powerful Delivery

Despite the proven importance of non-verbal communication, it is usually the words we use that we pay most attention to when we prepare – then the tonality or 'music' and *we hardly think about the non-verbal part at all.*

❖ **Dance:**

Non-verbal communication includes all of these aspects:

- Eye contact
- Posture
- Gestures

- Facial expressions
- Movement
- Energy

Eye contact. Always keep eye contact with your audience and not the screen behind you, the floor, the space above their heads or anywhere else. Keep having conversations with individuals throughout in different parts of the audience (rather than visually skimming the group) – 4-5 seconds each so they don't feel overwhelmed.

Facial expressions Be warm. Smile. Look like you are happy to be here. Learn to master your face, so you are using it to reinforce your words. Watch actors to see how they do this all the time to communicate their emotion (watch TV with the sound down to really get this).

Posture – ironically what feels wrong looks right and what feels right looks wrong - so you may want to get feedback or film yourself to assess your posture. Try to keep an open stance as much as possible, arms uncrossed, show your palms, keep a symmetrical stance with your weight slightly forward.

Movement and stage anchoring – this is where you use certain parts of the stage or space you are presenting in to make certain points or to signify certain ideas. So, for example, you may refer to 'The Past' by walking to the left of your space; the 'The Present' in the middle space and 'The Future' in the right-hand space (from the audience's view). This is very powerful at helping people to get your context, especially if you want to refer back to the ideas you stage-marked before.

Gestures - try to gesture naturally rather than theatrically – although for larger audiences you need larger gestures. Use your hands, as you would in normal conversation, for emphasis or appeal, and then return them to your 'holding position'.

Energy – your levels of physical energy will come from feeling engaged, enthusiastic or really positive about your subject. So connect with your passion for your subject before you go on.

❖ Music

Your voice creates the 'music' for your presentation and helps you to keep the energy up in your presentation, based on what I call the **4Ps:**

- Pace
- Pitch
- Pause
- Projection

Pace: Try not to go to fast – particularly when you feel nervous - by consciously slowing down without losing energy to your voice. Aim to vary the pace for dramatic effect to convey your range of emotion.

Pitch: This is about contrast - light and shade – loud and soft. You want to use your voice to amplify certain key points and convey warmth.

Pause: Pausing is incredibly powerful in presenting – particularly to add emphasis to an important point. So often, particularly when we are nervous, we can forget to pause or not pause for long enough. If you pause, it breaks your rhythm and the audience is attuned to really listen to what comes next. Notice, next time you experience a good presenter how often they pause for effect or before an important idea.

Projection: You need to project, particularly if you don't have a microphone – so you can be heard at the back and keep the energy strong in your voice.

Also, be precise about your speech – try to get rid of the filler words like basically, err, umm, obviously, actually, you know – because these will detract from your authority as a presenter and can sound fumbled. Always try to use pauses instead of filler noises. The first step though is to be aware you do it, which is where filming yourself or getting feedback can be useful.

If you want to play with non verbal meaning, have a go at asking the following question, and using the same words make your meaning sarcastic/ curious / worried / rude / respectful / kind:

Are you sure?

❖ Words

Words also provide a sense of music through phrasing, repetition and the power of 'three'.

Many famous speeches, such as Martin Luther King's 'I Have A Dream'; and Winston Churchill's 'We Shall Fight Them On The Beaches' made clever use of repetition. Abraham Lincoln's 'of the people, by the people, for the people' had a musical rhythm through its use of phrasing.

You may have built in some of these ideas when you prepared your content, but it is also worth reviewing how you can use these ideas to enhance your phrasing or rhythm when you come to rehearse your delivery.

Clear diction is obviously important in your delivery of your words – so you are clearly understood. Again, getting video feedback can be useful here.

Also, be mindful of your choice of words, the effect they may have on your audience and which words you want to stress in your delivery.

❖ Rehearsing and getting feedback

Given the significance of your non-verbal communication (your music and dance), you may find it useful to practice them – and even script in stage directions – when you come to rehearsing.

Feedback can be invaluable and the 'checklist' on p82 may be helpful to use for feedback. You can also use the list as a reminder to yourself of the key points to remember about good delivery.

Know Your Links

To sound really professional you need to be familiar with your links – how you will introduce the next idea while you are still finishing the previous idea - and make sure you have rehearsed these well, particularly if you are using slides.

You need to know what slide is coming next so that you can introduce your point before clicking through to that slide. This is far more professional than clicking through first and then allowing the slide to introduce the next point.

Performance Checklist

Presence/energy/charisma

Use of visual aids/props

Use of notes/cue cards

Powerful opener/engage immediately

Rapport with audience/involvement

Eye contact/non-verbal communication

Posture/gestures/movement

Vocal skill – 5 Ps (pace, pause, pitch, phrasing, projection)

Structure/roadmap

Effective storytelling – STARS

Handling of questions

Powerful ending/close

Key messages communicated?

Time keeping

❖ Handling questions

The key here is anticipation, which we covered in Session 2 and the importance of considering what questions are likely to come up.

When you are asked a question, particularly if you are presenting to a large group, you should repeat the question so that everyone is involved in hearing the answer.

If you don't the know the answer to a question, you have options as to how you handle it, but never fake it and pretend to know the answer if you don't. It is important to remain confident and not to let a question throw you off balance.

If you have anticipated well, there will not be many questions that you are unprepared for but here are a few ideas on answering questions that you find hard to answer:

- acknowledge that you don't know the answer or have the facts to hand and offer to get back to them

- throw the question out to the audience by acknowledging it is a good question and asking what other people in the room think about it. This can also buy you thinking time about *your* answer as you get other's opinions

- if you are asked a question that you haven't anticipated, that you would reasonably be assumed to know the answer to... but don't – then it is best to be honest rather than trying to cover up. People forgive knowledge gaps quicker than they forgive dishonesty, which they will usually pick up if you try to 'wing' it.

❖ Follow-up and Review (after your presentation)

Follow-up is often neglected but is usually very important to achieving the outcome you wanted from your presentation.

If you are going to follow-up, it is useful to have some means to contact people in the audience after the event – either by getting a list of delegates from the organizer or even asking people to leave a card so that you can keep in touch. Some presenters will even offer an incentive of a 'prize draw' to the winning business card to encourage people to leave a card.

If your presentation is a competitive pitch or tender, you will want to get feedback about your presentation – particularly if you are not successful in winning the bid. This can be invaluable for the next time you present.

Make a habit of reviewing your own performance each time you present. There may even be someone in the audience who can give you some honest feedback – a team member or colleague perhaps. You want to review on the basis of considering these 2 aspects:

1. What did I like about my presentation? What went well, that I am pleased about? What would I want to repeat in future presentations?

2. What would I do differently next time? What adjustments would make my presentation even better next time?

<u>Over To You</u>: Get ready so you can deliver with confidence

You are nearly there.

You need to **learn your words**, using the **4-step process** and **mentally prepare**, using the 3 exercises we covered. If you can, get feedback from your rehearsal so you can make any necessary changes. **Anticipate questions** that are likely to come up and you can also rehearse your answers. Finally, decide if you will **follow-up** and whether you need to build in some way of getting contact details for the audience.

...and then you will be ready to give this presentation.

Afterword

My story

I started my career in public relations. As a young, junior member of the team, I felt very self-conscious and uncomfortable whenever I had to speak in presentations or client meetings.

The problem was, as I became more senior in my career, my dislike of presenting and public speaking stuck – and the gap between my seniority and my ability to present or speak in public became a big issue.

One of the worst moments was when, as an Account Director at Ogilvy & Mather, I was asked to present the PR proposals to one of our clients. I arrived at the meeting, expecting to be presenting to a few people and was ushered in to a large hall where around 50 expectant faces watched me as I walked on to the stage. I was horror struck. I would like to say that I got through it, I managed to present despite my initial shock… but that wasn't how it went.

I stood on the stage, and instead of thinking about my opening, my brain was repeatedly reminding me that my worst nightmare was happening: I was dying on stage. It was 20 minutes of hell. I coped, but I decided that I needed to overcome my dread of speaking in public and learn how to do this well.

I read extensively, I interviewed some great presenters, I studied and observed and most importantly, I presented as much as I could. I started small, in groups or situations that felt relatively comfortable and yet kept stretching myself to take on opportunities to practice.

I think the key thing for me was understanding what makes a presentation work: how to structure your content so your audience absorb and remember your message, how to get into rapport and involve your audience, how to add interest to your content. Once you have this basic understanding, it is far less daunting to have a go at putting it into practice. That is what I hope this book will have given you. The basic technique and information to give you the foundations to get presenting as often as you can.

So now it is over to you.

Try to use every opportunity you have to give a presentation – although it may seem time-consuming or daunting at times (particularly as the stakes get higher), it is the only way to get *really* good at this. Those presenters you admire are the ones who have stuck at it. I wish you every success with your next presentation (and every presentation you give after that…).

Help! I've got a presentation coming up...

If you want to take your skill further and get more help with your presentation, you can contact me to arrange a one-to-one coaching session to address any areas of your preparation, content or delivery.

I meet clients in the North West of England, but can also support you online from anywhere in the world.

Contact me with a brief message about your presentation needs and I will be in touch:

Email:	caroline@lovepresenting.com
Web:	lovepresenting.com
Phone:	0151 327 3845